Life Love & You

LOUISE LINGER HOWE

Copyright © 2016 Louise Linger Howe
All rights reserved
First Edition

PAGE PUBLISHING, INC.
New York, NY

First originally published by Page Publishing, Inc. 2016

ISBN 978-1-68289-619-8 (pbk)
ISBN 978-1-68289-620-4 (digital)

Printed in the United States of America

To everyone on the planet: I am dedicating this book to you.

Whatever you do, I wrote this for you. I am going to make it simple, short, and to the point as I can because I know how busy everyone is. So let's get started.

Love Your Life

Love your life…
It's a gift from God!
Take care of your body… it's the only one you got
Show appreciation…
To the people who deserve it.
Don't take people or things for granted,
You never know what can happen
Just be nice!
It will make people HAPPY.
SMILE…

Now
Get on with life

—Louise Linger Howe

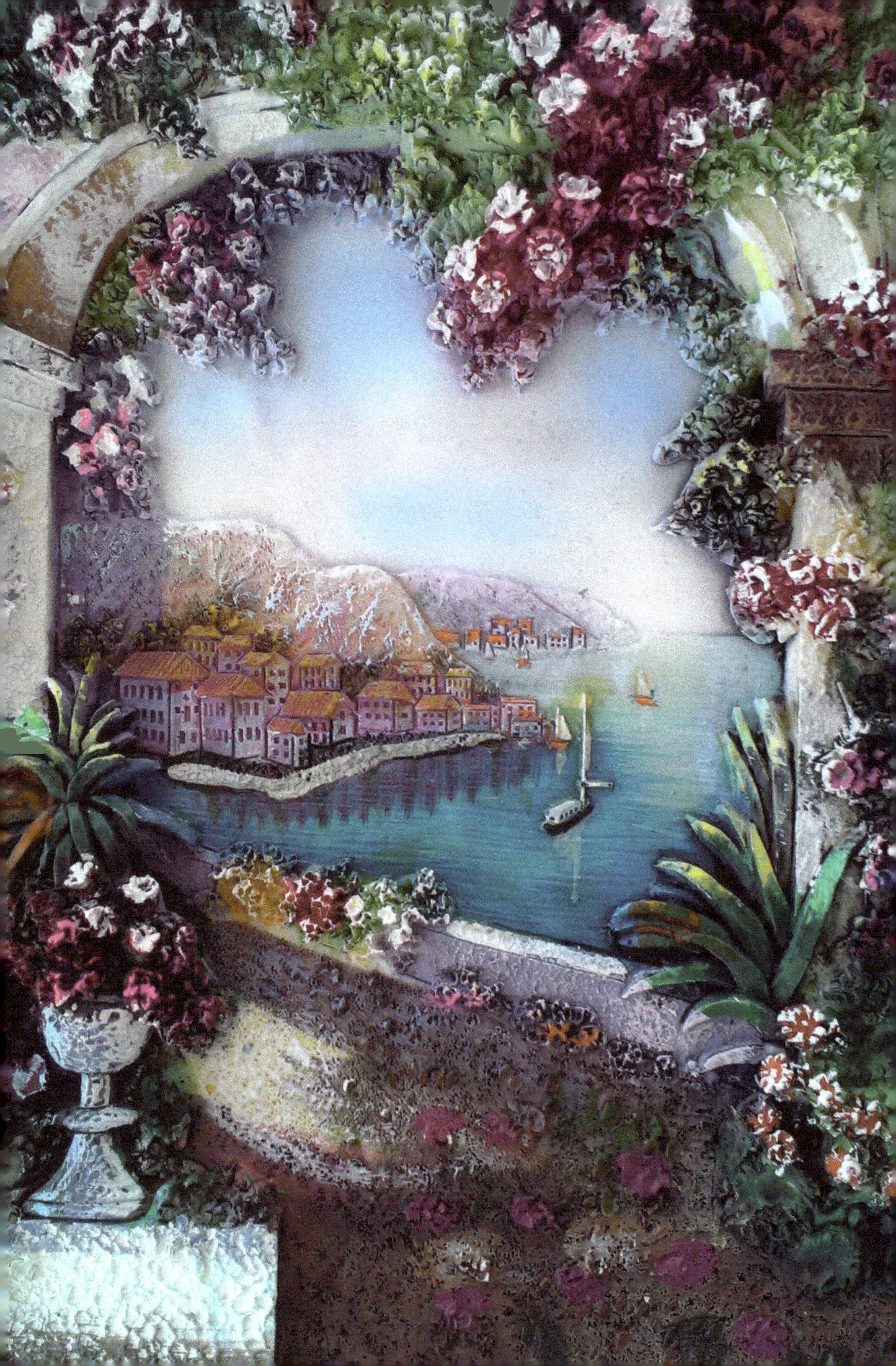

Gift to God

There's just no easy answer
For the mess that were all in
It's all because of greed
And now we find we're suffering

If we could all just work together
And figure it all out
The world would be a better place
Believe me there's no doubt

The longer we go on like this
The harder it will be
To make the changes that we need
For peace and harmony

Everyone's so angry
Frustrated, feeling sad
Wondering what life's all about
We just don't have a plan

If this is life, there's something wrong
We can't go on like this
We got to keep on reaching out
And make more sense of it

God really does have all the answers
If only we could see
That life could really change
For us and make us all happy

So what are we really
Waiting for the answers in our heart
We do have the choice to choose
To make a brand new start

Start the day by giving
Thanks and be grateful you're alive
To love your life and
Cherish it

Now that's your gift
To God!

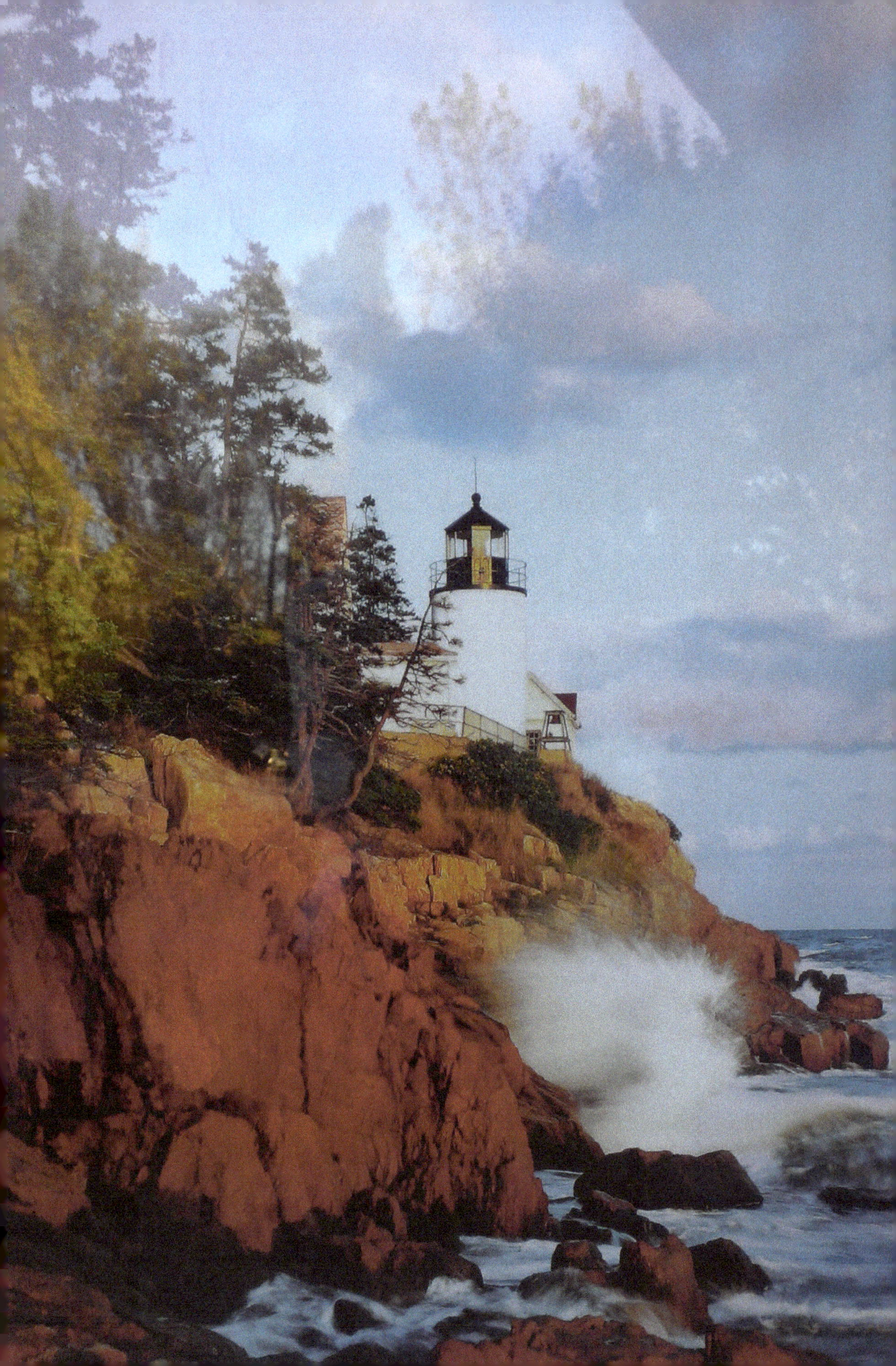

PAY ATTENTION

Pay Attention

We live in a time where there are so many distractions. So many things going on around us. We are starting to zone out, not paying attention to what is really going on around us. Maybe the more we're getting connected, the more we are getting disconnected. Disconnected to what's really important, like being a loving, caring, respectful, honest, grateful, and a thankful person.

Every day we have to work on being the best person we can be and sometimes that becomes a not so easy task. But we all have a choice.

We all have the choice to choose the person we want to be, and the life we want to live. And sometimes it's the not knowing that we have the power and control, we own it. But that's where self-control comes in because we have to practice self-control. Whether it's drinking, eating, gambling, shopping, or sex I think you get the picture. And only we can be the enforcer over our control. But what is it about us? We keep searching for answers outside ourselves. Yet we hold the key because we know for darn sure that if we do not want to do something; we are just not going to do it. We have got to be a little more open-minded to change. If we keep doing the same thing and it's not working out, we're going to keep getting the same results, back to square one. And then on top of that, there's that blame game. And as one of my teachers at school said, point your finger to others and the other fingers point right back to you. There's also a saying out there that says, "You are not considered a failure until you start blaming other people." And as you know, we live in a world filled with blamers. When does it stop?

Let's all start today. Each and every one of us and let's not find excuses not to do it.

Take responsibility for what you say and do because actions speak louder than words. Which lead us to just do it for goodness sake. Just imagine if we all took control over ourselves. If we can control ourselves, we will be in a much better state of mind to help others physically, emotionally and spiritually. Oh yes! And the world will start getting into balance.

We need to treat people the way we would like to be treated. If you know it's wrong but everybody's doing it, do the right thing because that's what makes people good leaders; right now the world is a little short of them and some might say, what can I do? Work on yourself and help others to be strong then the domino effect can begin.

One person at a time. Put out as much positive energy in the universe as you can and we will be rewarded. The world is big enough for all of us to live. Let's start enjoying our life and stop hurting each other. Life's too short for that. The greed and wanting to have all the power has got to stop. Haven't we've been punished enough?

I am giving everyone an assignment. Start with yourself by writing down five things that you would like to change in yourself, to make you the best person you can be.

These are my five things

1. Love your life. It's a gift from God.
2. Take care of your body; it's the only one you got.
3. Show appreciation to the people who deserve it.
4. Don't take people or things for granted; you never know what can happen.
5. Just be Nice! It will make people happy.

Smile! Now get on with your life.

I've got this on my refrigerator as reminder of what's important, and to pay attention every day of what's going on in my life and what I can do to make it better.

LISTEN TO YOUR BODY

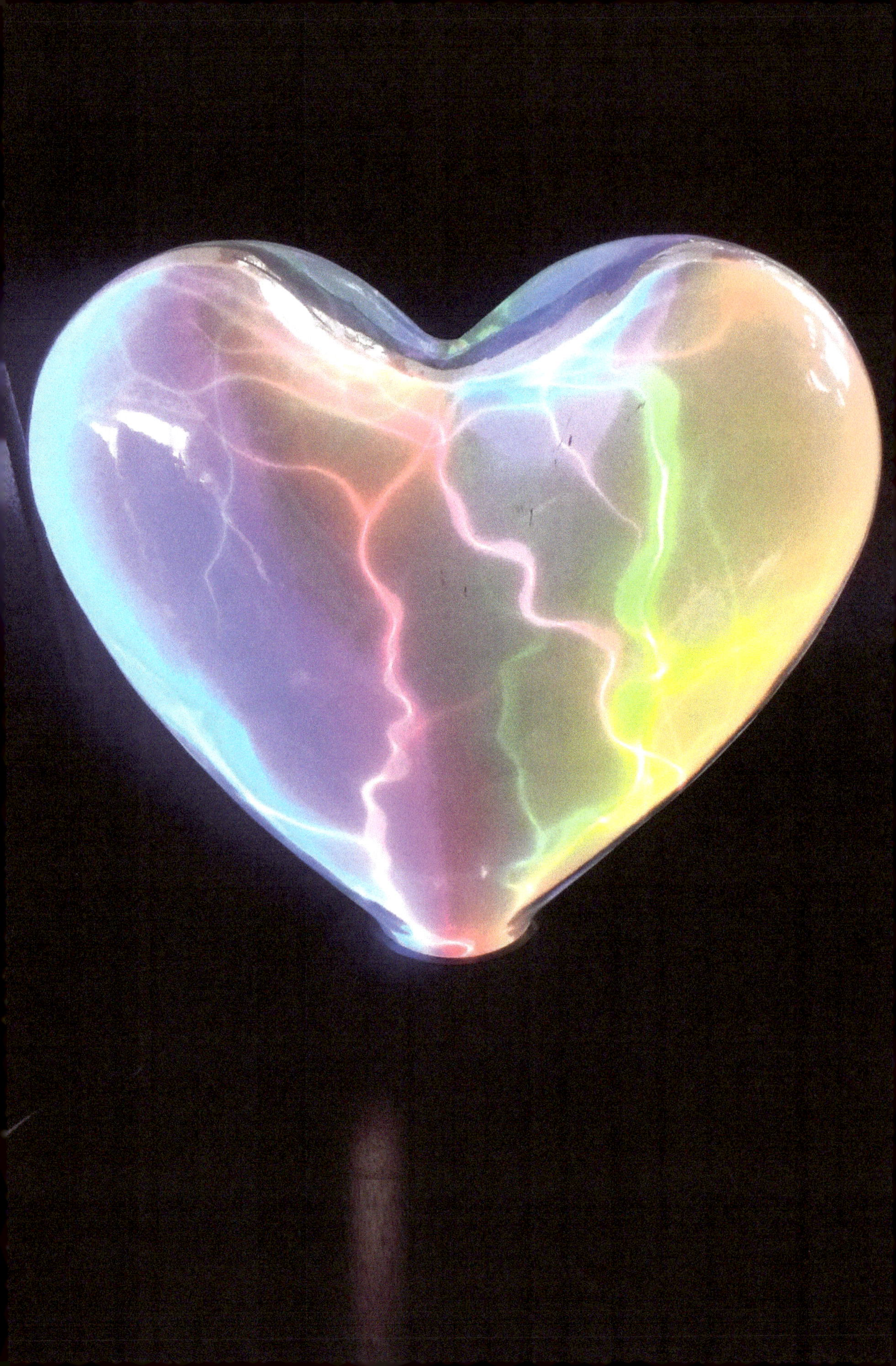

Listen to Your Body

Our bodies are amazing. We are walking and talking miracles. What our bodies are capable of doing is off the charts. And our brains, well, think about it, it's our built in computer; but we don't have to keep charging it up. We do need to maintain. Just like our car or if you own a pool; your car can't start if it doesn't have gas and look out if it runs out of oil and sometimes the car can start making weird noises. That's the car telling you something is going on and it's not good.

Our bodies talk to us every day; I'll give you the easy ones. Stomach growling from being hungry, sweating from being hot, and you know the next one—put a sweater on me, I'm cold.

And then there's the maintenance issue, the people who stop maintaining, not eating right, lack of sleep, smoking, stressed out, and no exercise. By this time, the body is probably yelling at you. The thing is, not to let it get to that point, that's where paying attention comes in. Listen to your body, and be the captain of your ship.

Be in charge of you. Take time out for yourself. When our grandmothers and mothers told us, "Eat your vegetables," "Stop and smell the roses," and "Don't cry over spilled milk," sums up a lot to your mind, body, and spirit. Vegetables do a body good. Smelling the roses is good for your spirit, soul, and for your mind. Don't stress out on things that already happened; there's nothing you can do about it. Just pick yourself up, and start a new day.

I'm very passionate about all of this because I see and hear a lot of people going to the doctor. I think some of them are looking for a magic pill that's going to solve all their health issues. But the magic is in us; we have the power and control. We control what we eat; it's up to us to stop smoking. We make the choice to exercise. Eat less sugar, drink more water. Maybe try meditating. And don't forget how important fruits and vegetables are.

Don't get me wrong, doctors are great if you fall and break a bone, or if you cut yourself and need stitches, or for delivering babies. Thank you, thank you, thank you, Doctors.

But here's where the "but" comes in, we can't go to them and say fix me when we are totally not taking care of ourselves. At least, give yourself a chance.

1. Be aware of what you're eating and what's in your food.
2. Don't go crazy, but drink a fair amount of water.
3. Less sugar, less sugar, less sugar, what can I say? It's the number one thing that ages the body.
4. Fried foods. For me, if I eat fried foods, my skin breaks out. That's my body talking to me, "don't do it."
5. Try to eat more alkaline foods which are almost all of your vegetables and fruits meat and cheese are high in the acid forming section.
6. De-stress. Talk to a friend, get a massage, soak in the tub, meditate, get connected with nature, sing, dance, or watch a comedy.

Now that you have done everything in your power to change, be honest with yourself. Are you living a healthy lifestyle? Are you the captain of your ship? Are you listening to your body? And are you paying attention to all the wonderful things we feel when we are connected with this unlimited, free energy that surrounds us, that has been given to use from our beloved creator, God?

How wonderful!

FIVE THINGS TO THINK ABOUT

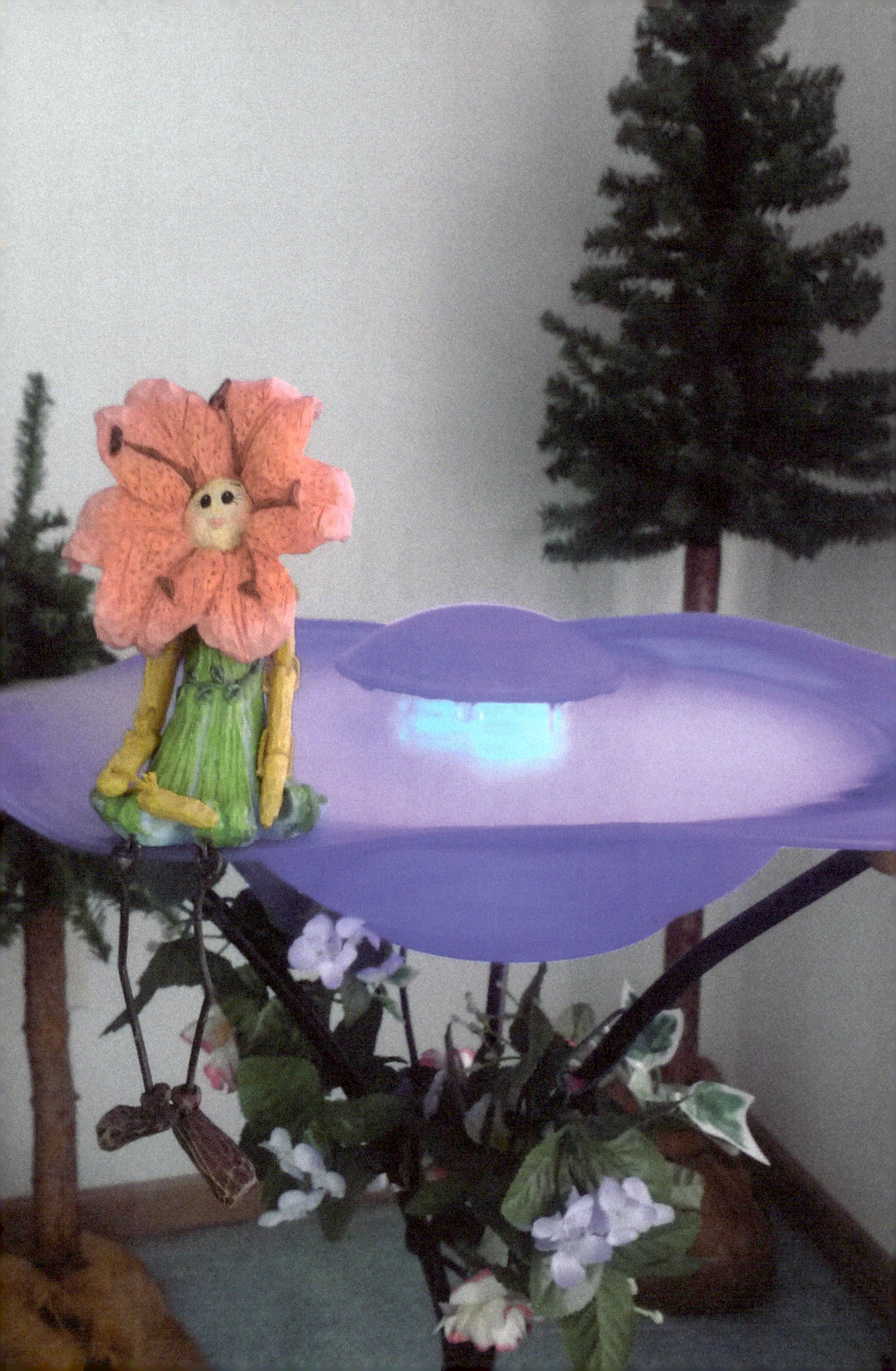

1. The truth hurts.

We have all heard about selective hearing. Well, maybe we're listening, but only to the things we want to hear; because a lot of us don't want to hear the truth. For some of us, the truth hurts. But sometimes, those "hurts" could be lessons that we need to learn. These are the lessons you can't learn at school or from books; these are lessons of life. Every day we are learning and growing just from the people that are around us. We can also learn from other people's mistakes. None of us is perfect. We are all a work in progress. But it's when we are not learning from our mistakes and continue the same pattern; and when people confront us about it, we don't want to hear it, oh yes! Because sometimes, the truth hurts. It's important that we are honest with ourselves; honest enough to realize that if we truly want to change. Anything is possible and we have everything to gain. So stop, look, and listen. Stop the selective hearing. Start looking at the big picture and listen whole heartedly on what people have to say. You just might learn something about yourself, something you yourself just haven't realized. It's all a learning experience, so never stop learning and embrace the challenges.

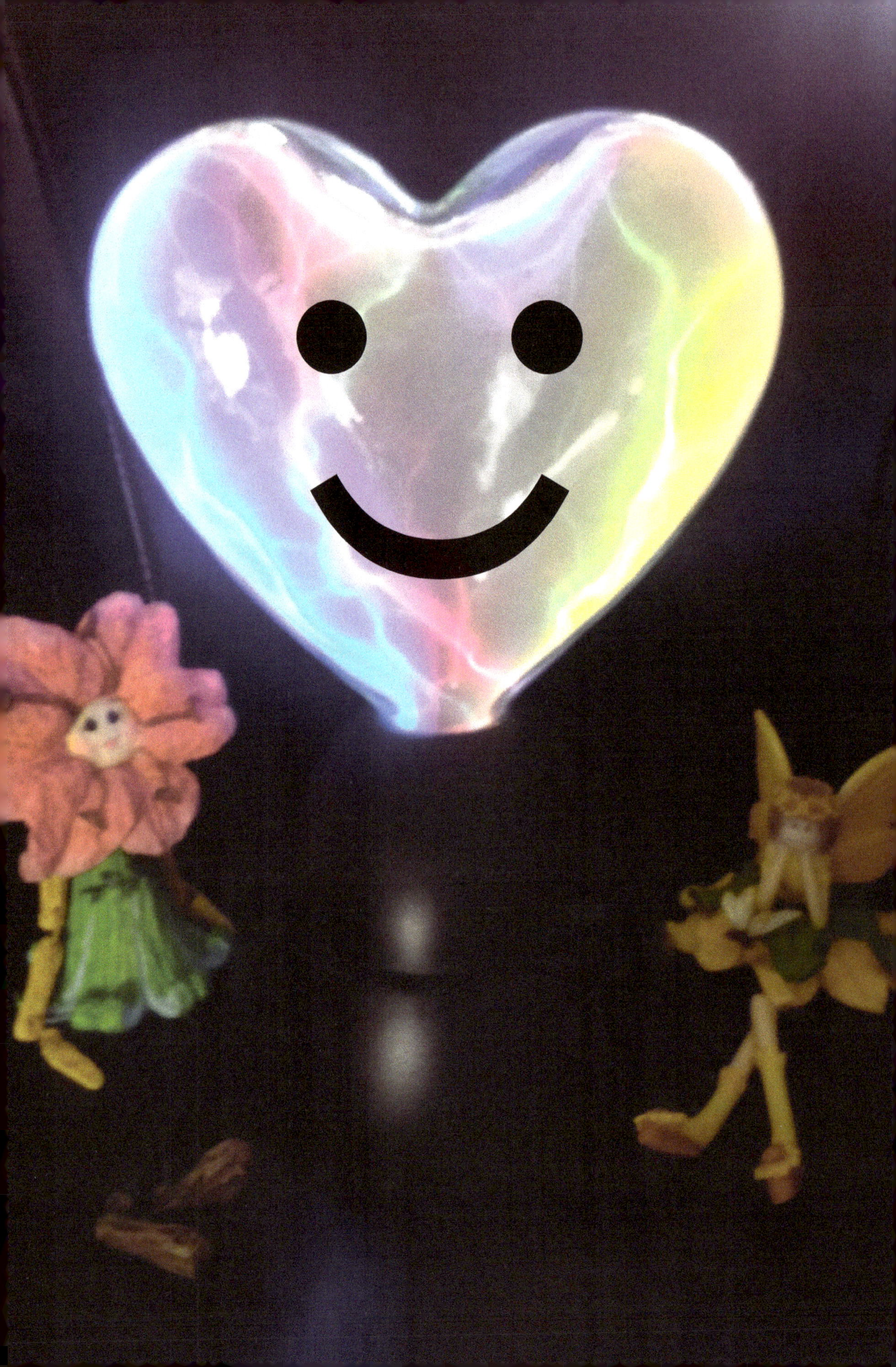

2. Not everyone is going to like you.

Not everyone is going to like you. Get over it. This is a biggie. Sometimes, we try to please people by doing everything we can to get them to like us, and find out that no matter what we do or say, it ain't going to happen. But that's okay because there are plenty of people out there who will like and love you. So invest your time and energy on them. Stop beating yourself up from people who will not reciprocate to you. Nobody wants to be in a one-sided relationship anyway. So I say: move out, move on, move along; because there is nothing more draining than a relationship that's not going anywhere.

Don't set yourself up just to be knocked down. It will save you a lot of hurt and frustration.

But let's not forget that each and every one of us is special in our own way. And sometimes it's just an individual taste. But know that you are beautiful to someone. Smile. ☺ God loves you.

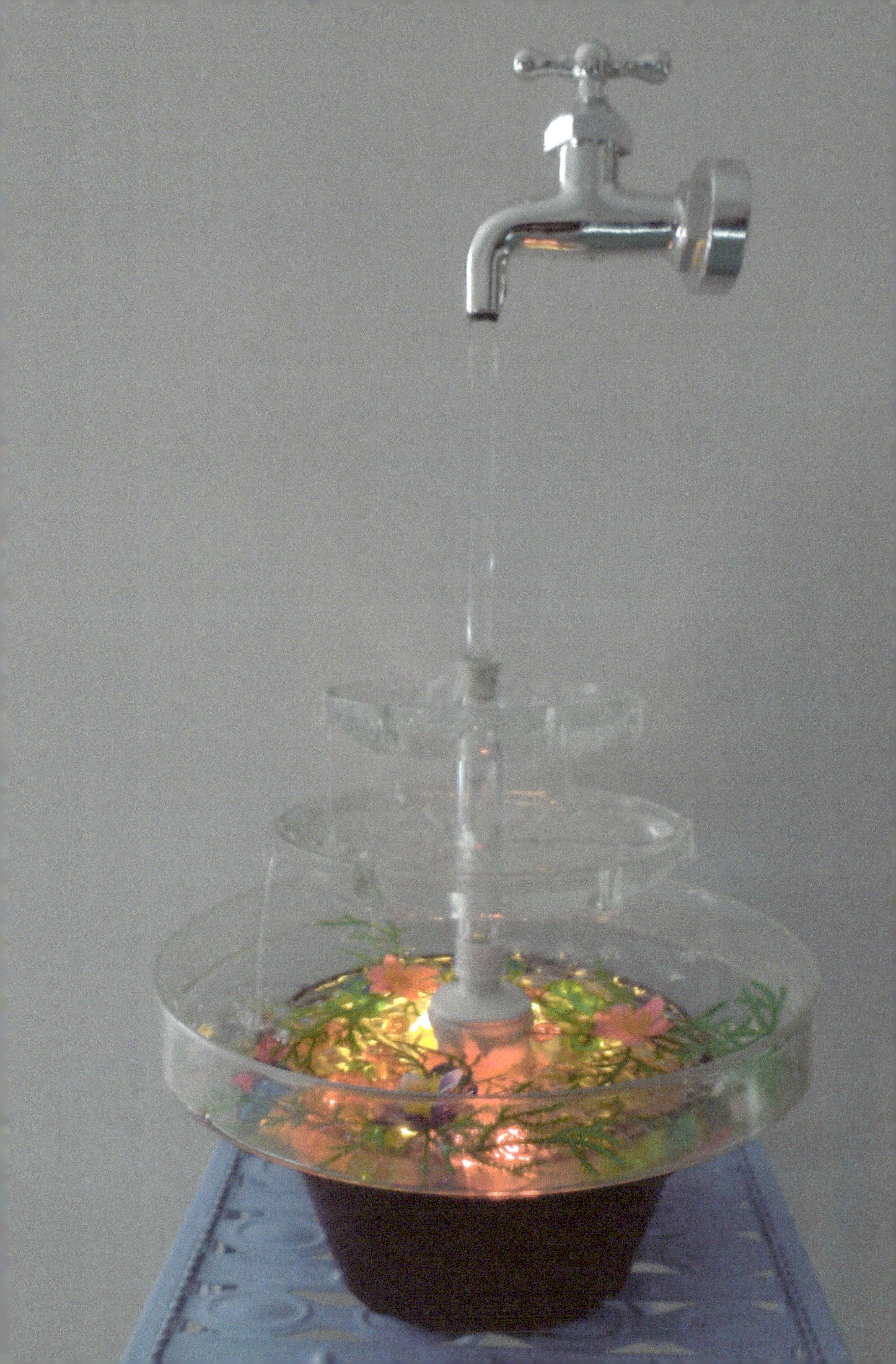

3. Don't try to figure it out.

Everyone knows the saying, "It is what it is." That's just another form of saying; don't try to figure it out. We spend so much of our time asking why did this person do this? Why did this person say that? Why did this happen? And why did that happen? Why? Why? Why? Then, we start thinking, analyzing, and replay scenarios. But think about it when we watch a ball game and we see them replaying the play. Well, they can replay it a hundred times; the end result is the same. It's not going to change the outcome by watching it over and over again. Sometimes there is no figuring it out. Sometimes things just happen and sometimes things weren't meant to be; or maybe it's just not our day or year. So let's stop wasting our energy on trying to figure it out. Because, yes, it is what it is.

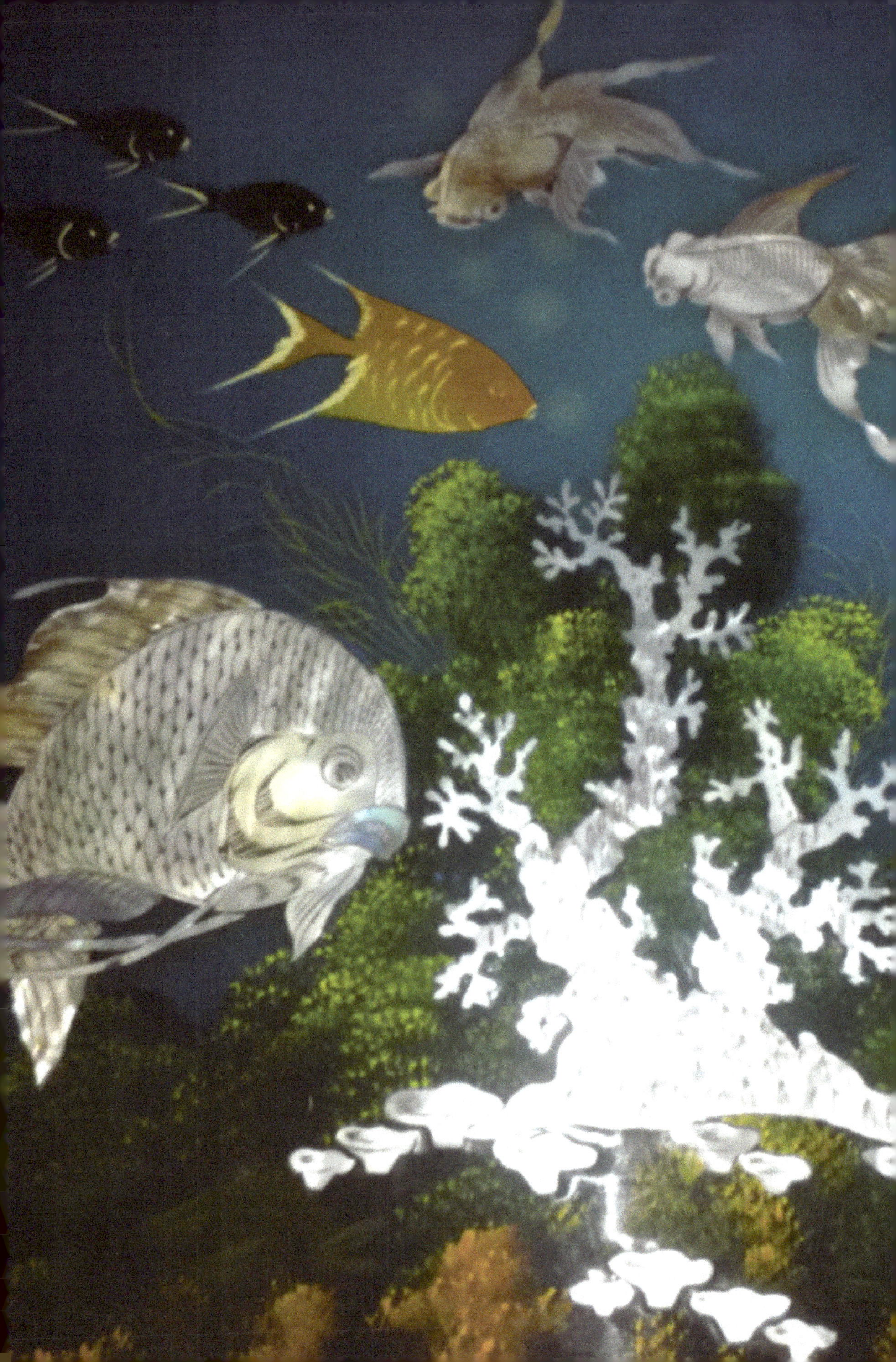

4. Stop worrying about what other people think.

If you are trying to be the best person you can be, and you are a loving, caring, grateful and thankful person; does it really matter what others think? People are always going to be saying something and a lot of times those somethings aren't even true. I say, imagine how boring life would be if we all looked the same, acted the same, wore the same clothes, did all the same things. It's okay to be different providing you're not hurting anyone. Being different can make you a unique, interesting, special person. What I'm saying is, you're not boring. That's what makes life a lot more interesting for you and the other people around you because you are giving them something to talk about. But that's okay because you're just dancing to the beat of a different drum. And some people might even be a little jealous of that.

But when people talk about you, and say some bad things about you, things that aren't even true. You cannot keep dwelling on that. Because every time you do, you will keep reinfecting the wound and you need to give yourself a chance to heal.

If you have to take one full day of being upset, crying, getting angry—because first we get hurt and then we get angry—so get it out. Get it all out of your system but only under one condition:

That when you get up the next day. You say I am a changed person. I am not going to let people hurt me. I am strong. I can handle their criticism. I chose to be happy.

Whatever they say just flows over me, the negativity does not attach itself to me anymore. I will limit my exposure to them.

But I will always be there if they need me because I have become a stronger and better person because of this.

Because now I have become untouchable to their "hurts."

Remind yourself to practice this saying daily:

> I am strong
> I am in control
> I choose to be happy
> I love life and life loves me
> I have become a magnet
> For attracting love, harmony
> And peace, within my
> Mind, body, and soul

And I know that God is here for me!

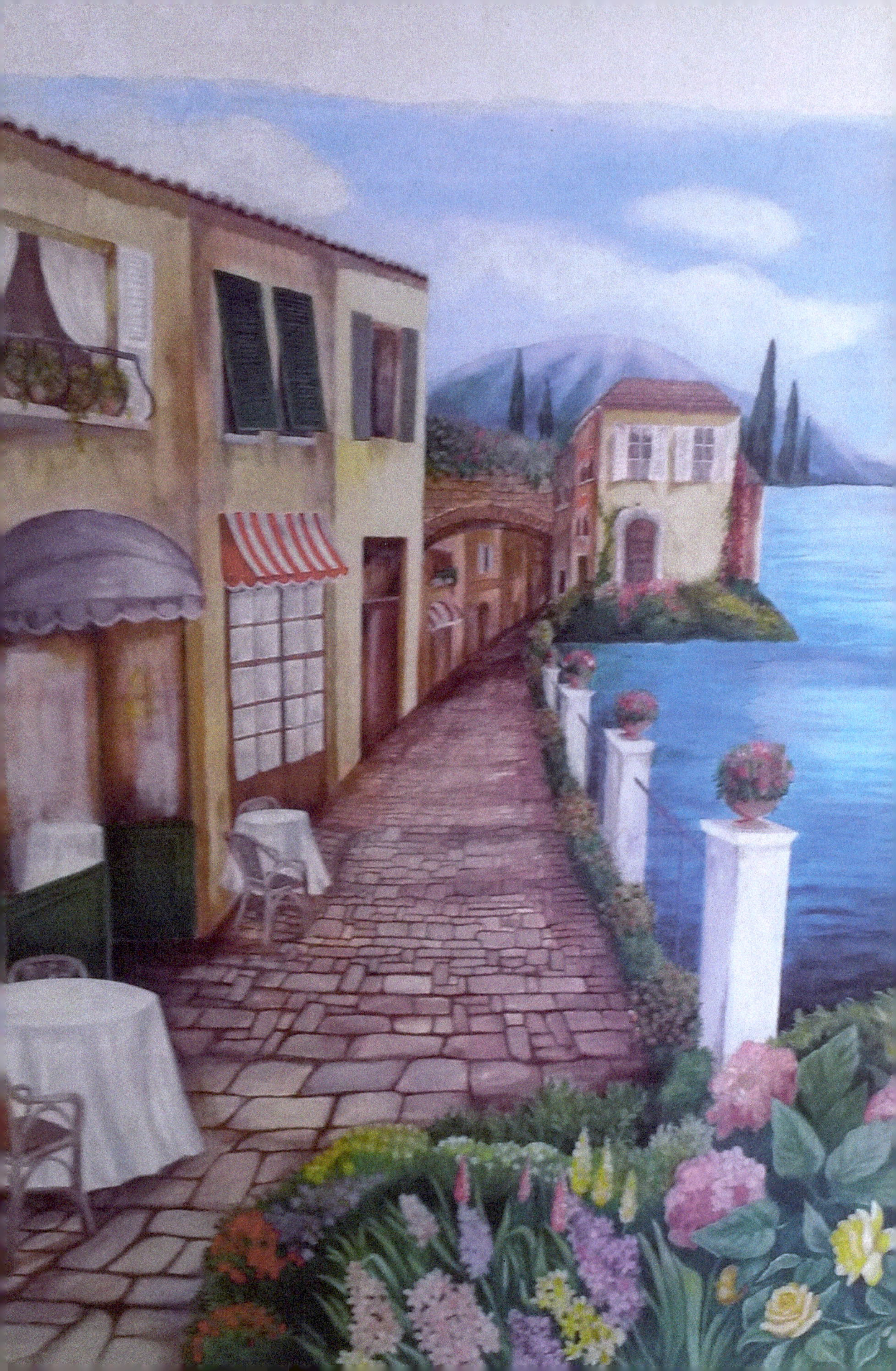

5. You can't change people.

I saved the best one for last. You can<u>not</u> change people. So word to the wise, don't waste your time trying, it ain't gonna happen. Sometimes we see people doing very destructive things and things we know are going to hurt them. But really there is very little we can do. We can offer some advice, present them with options and make some suggestion but that's it.

It's their life and they have got to learn it for themselves. Some people have got to learn it the hard way, and some people just don't get it.

But we have got to accept this, we don't have to like it; we have to accept it. Because it's their life, it's their journey, it's the path that they want to take. Just don't get dragged down that path with them.

That's where we have got to take a stand and say enough is enough. You can only help a person out for so long. Then we have got to stand up for ourselves because we have our life to live. We can't change them but we have the power to change ourselves and how we handle the situation.

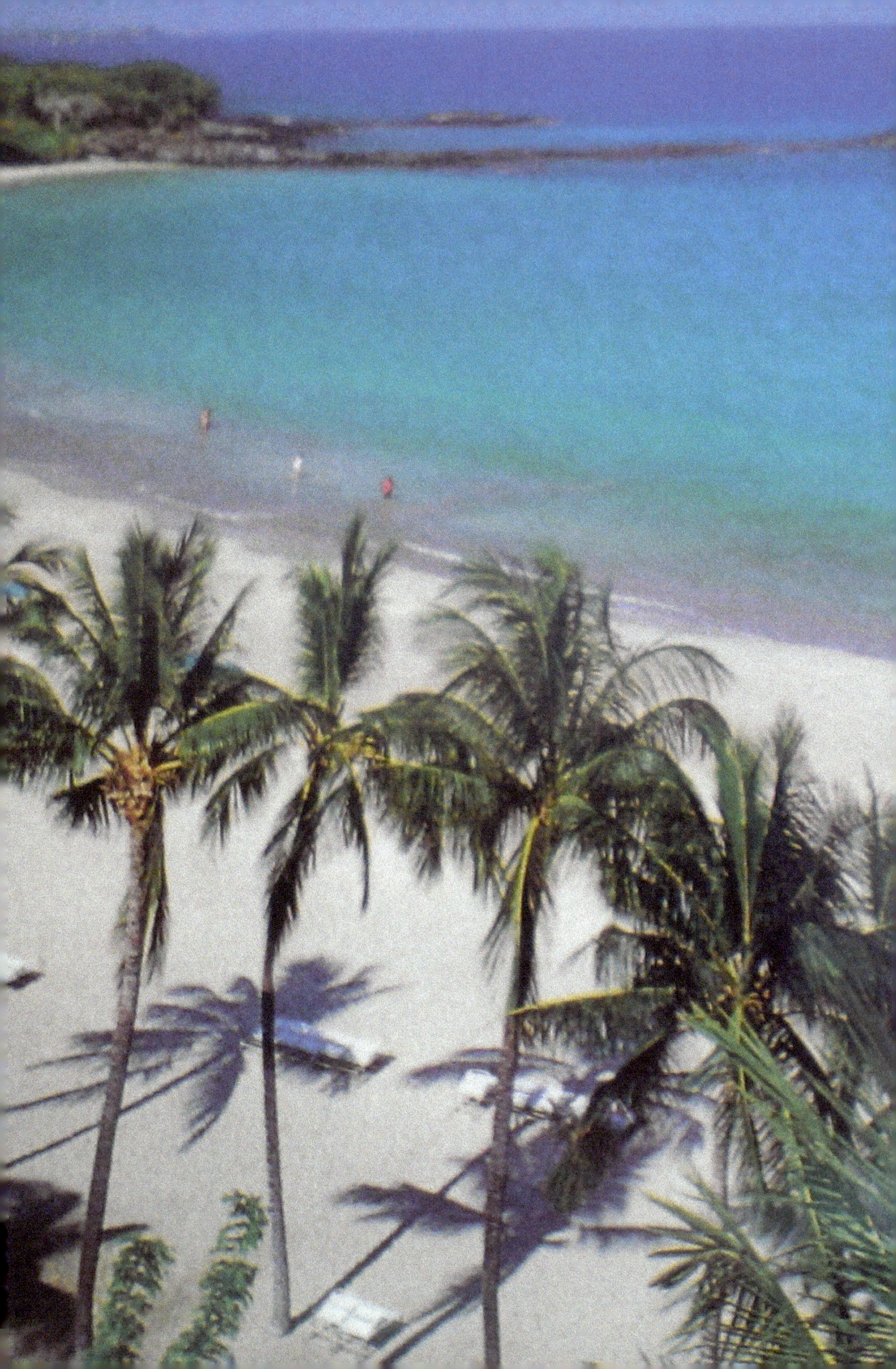

CREATE YOUR OWN PARADISE

Create Your Own Paradise

This is an interesting one because everyone has their own vision of what paradise means to them. But this is a very important one. It's a great stress reliever. For some people it's a beautiful ocean view. For some, it might be a breathtaking garden with all the incredible scent of the flowers, it could be a flowing waterfall, or the sun setting behind the mountains.

Now, bring that fabulous vision inside your home by a scenic picture of your choosing or, possibly, putting fresh cut flowers in a vase on your table. Paint some of the rooms in your house in bright cheery colors. Put a small fountain in the corner of the room. Be creative and have fun with it. So on those days where you just had a real bad day.

You know that you have created a little paradise in the privacy of your own home, and as Dorothy in the Wizard of Oz said, "There's no place like home."

So sit back, distress, and enjoy the beautiful surroundings inside and out. Outside what God has created and inside what you have created.

And for those of you who are good with visualization you don't have to buy a thing. Just close your eyes and create your own paradise in your mind. Wow!

It's all good!

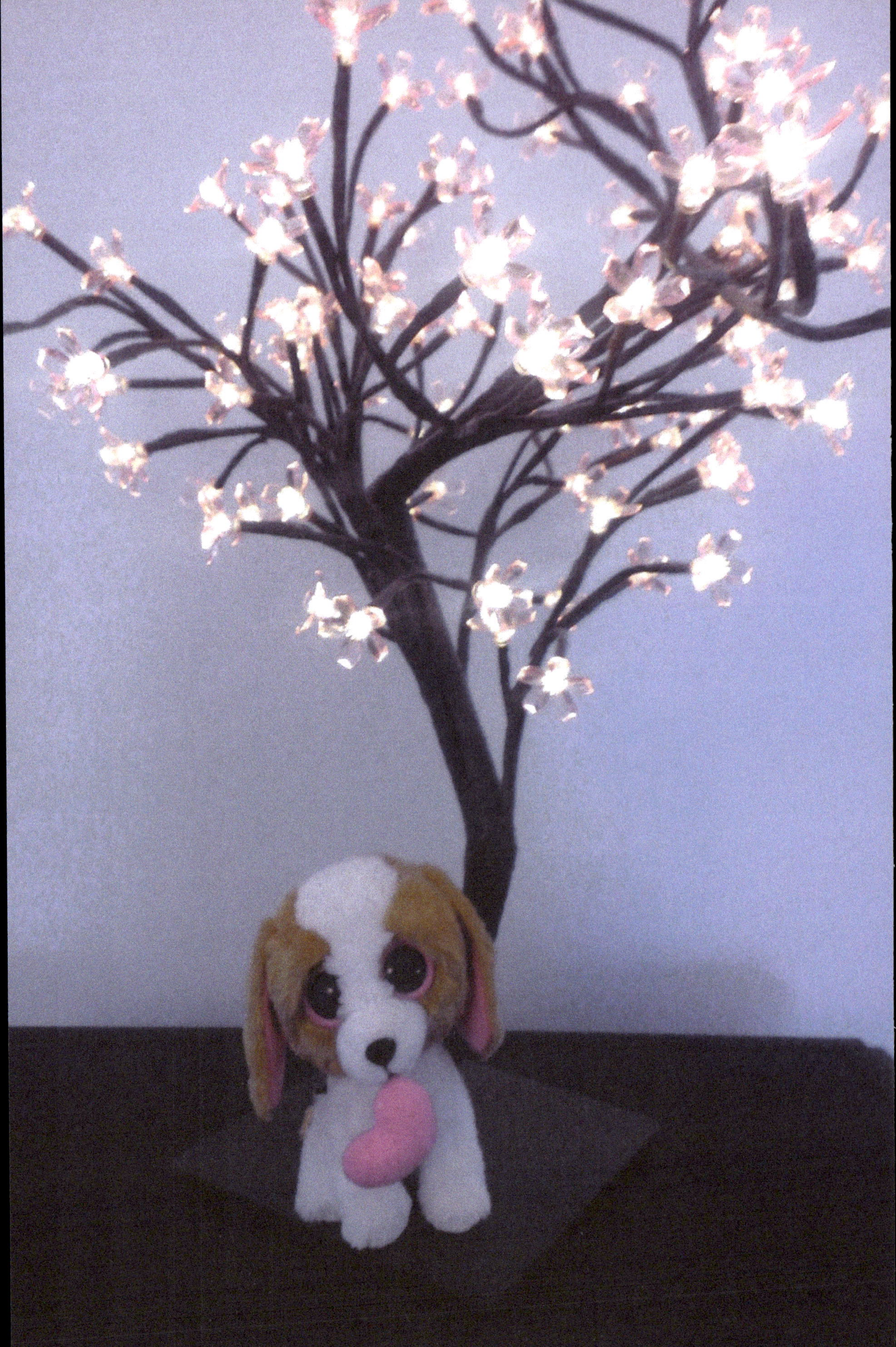

GOD WORKS IN MYSTERIOUS WAYS

Pets

All I can say is, if you live alone or lonely; can't have children, pets can sure fill that void. When they say a dog is man's best friend. They are truly right. I have a Chihuahua, his name is Buddy, the perfect name for him by the way. He was a birthday present to my son, Paul, from his girlfriend at the time for his eighteenth birthday. I have to admit, I was not a happy camper. I thought who's going to take care of him? Who's going to take him out? What just happened? Well, my son was cute. Naive but cute. He said he loves to be in his house, I said really, as I hear cries coming from my son's room, where little Buddy was lying in his house. So I went in my son's room, opened up the gate to his house, and little Buddy was shaking and was very frightened as I picked him up. He looked up at me and kissed me. It was an instant attachment.

That's been fifteen years ago. He is a great watch dog. He's a great friend, he's my little Buddy.

We can also learn a lot from them. They want what all of us want. They want you to love them. And just by looking at them, you are rewarding them by giving them acknowledgment.

For my son, he move out, got married, and no, he was not taking little buddy. That wasn't going to happen.

This is my story. How God works in mysterious ways. God was very creative. He knew we would not ever have gotten a dog on our own. So he brought little buddy into our lives by my son; getting this awesome birthday present by a sweet young lady by the name of Katie.

And now by having a dog, I was able to experience the love this incredible animal can give you.

It's also interesting that, God, if you spell it backward, it spells d-o-g. I wonder if that was God's plan. Something to think about. Wouldn't you say?

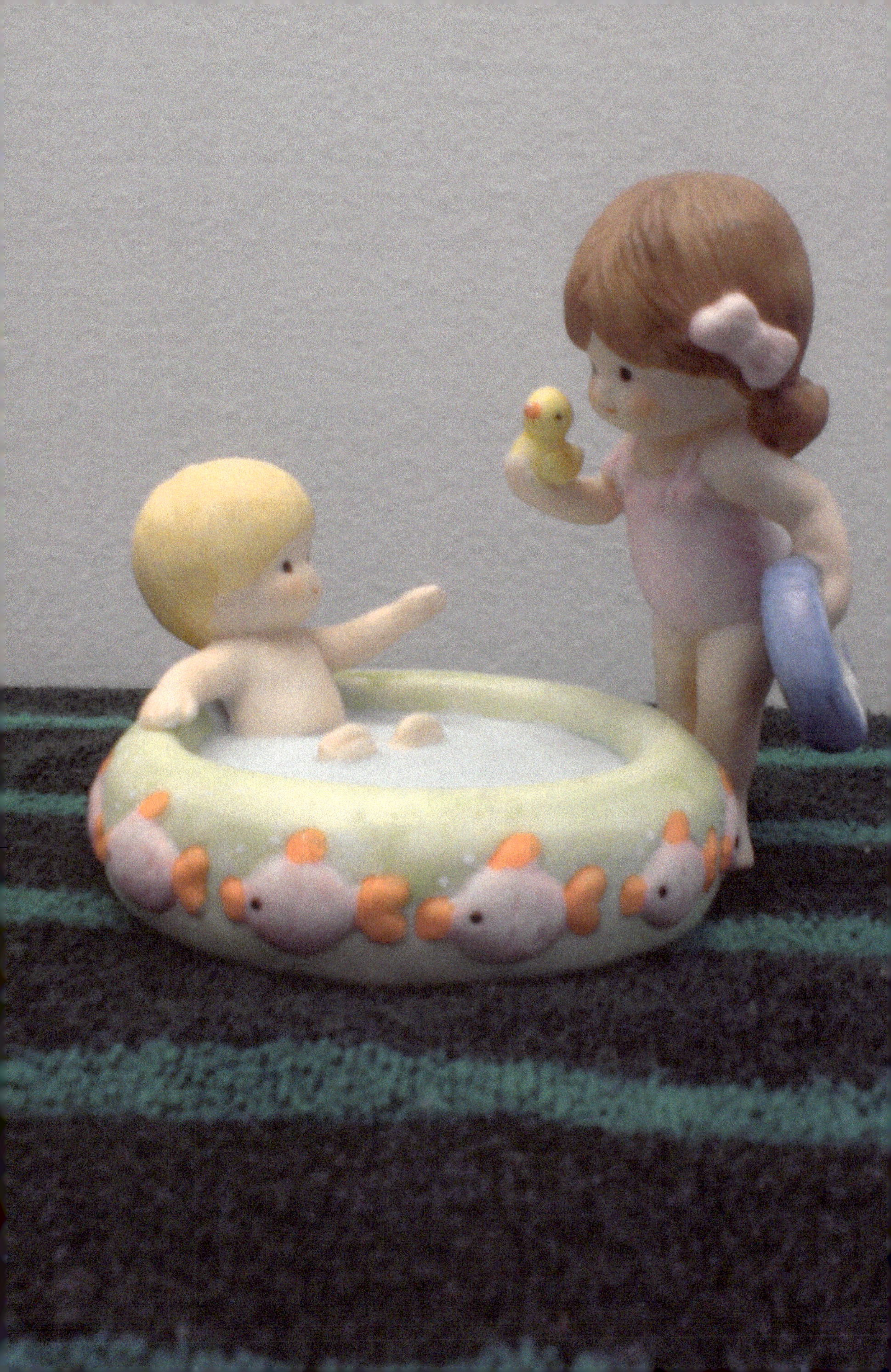

JUST BE NICE

Just Be Nice

Just imagine, if we lived in a world where everyone was just nice, it's plain, it's simple, it's not complicated, and it's three little words that go a long way. We should actually have a "Just Be Nice" day. Some people will probably say, "Well, I'm nice every day." Well, maybe just be extra nice. See where that takes you. Also image how less stressed we would be if people were just nice. But we also have to realize that there are people out there who are going through some hard times, maybe a death in the family, maybe it's financially, or maybe they're not feeling well. So to those people, we have got to be extra nice because someday we might need people to be extra nice to us.

The whole idea is putting positive vibes out there and maybe it will start rubbing off on others. So let's start smiling more, do some good deeds for others, and be nice to one another.

And let's try and make every day a "Just Be Nice" day. I don't think we can make it any simpler than that, so let's start trying it out on people, and let's see what happens.

You heard the saying, "Have a nice day." Well I can tell you if people are nice to you, you can almost guarantee that you are going to have a nice day.

It's us, it's the people that make the difference. So let's start generating it all across the world!

Just Be Nice

Then maybe people across the world will want to join the club (the just be nice club), and the ones who don't, well they will surely be missing out—because that's a big part of people being happy. When you are around nice people, it will make you happy. Now, that's something to smile about.

Smile you are beautiful!

Music Is Magic

It's amazing how you could be feeling down, or you had a rough day and then a song comes on the radio, and like magic it can amazingly lift you up, turn your mood totally around like the click of a switch—your spirits become incredibly lifted. Isn't it wonderful when that happens?

Whatever kind of music does that to you, make it a point to listen to that magical music. That's what also keeps the heart and soul young.

I love all kinds of music. I have music to dance to, sing to, music to clean house to, and music to relax to. I could not image a world without it, could you?

So when you have those days, when you need a little pep in your step, turn it on, and the magic will begin. It's fun, it's free, and it's natural—no drugs here. It's just an incredible fantastic feeling that makes you want to dance and sing, and you feel like you can almost do anything.

Some say music is like medicine. Yes, it truly is, but without all the harmful side effect, the only effect you will feel is the feeling of just feeling great. It's the mind and body experience. So experience it for yourself and let the magic begin. So turn it on, and turn it up.

Add some Rock 'n' Roll
to your soul.

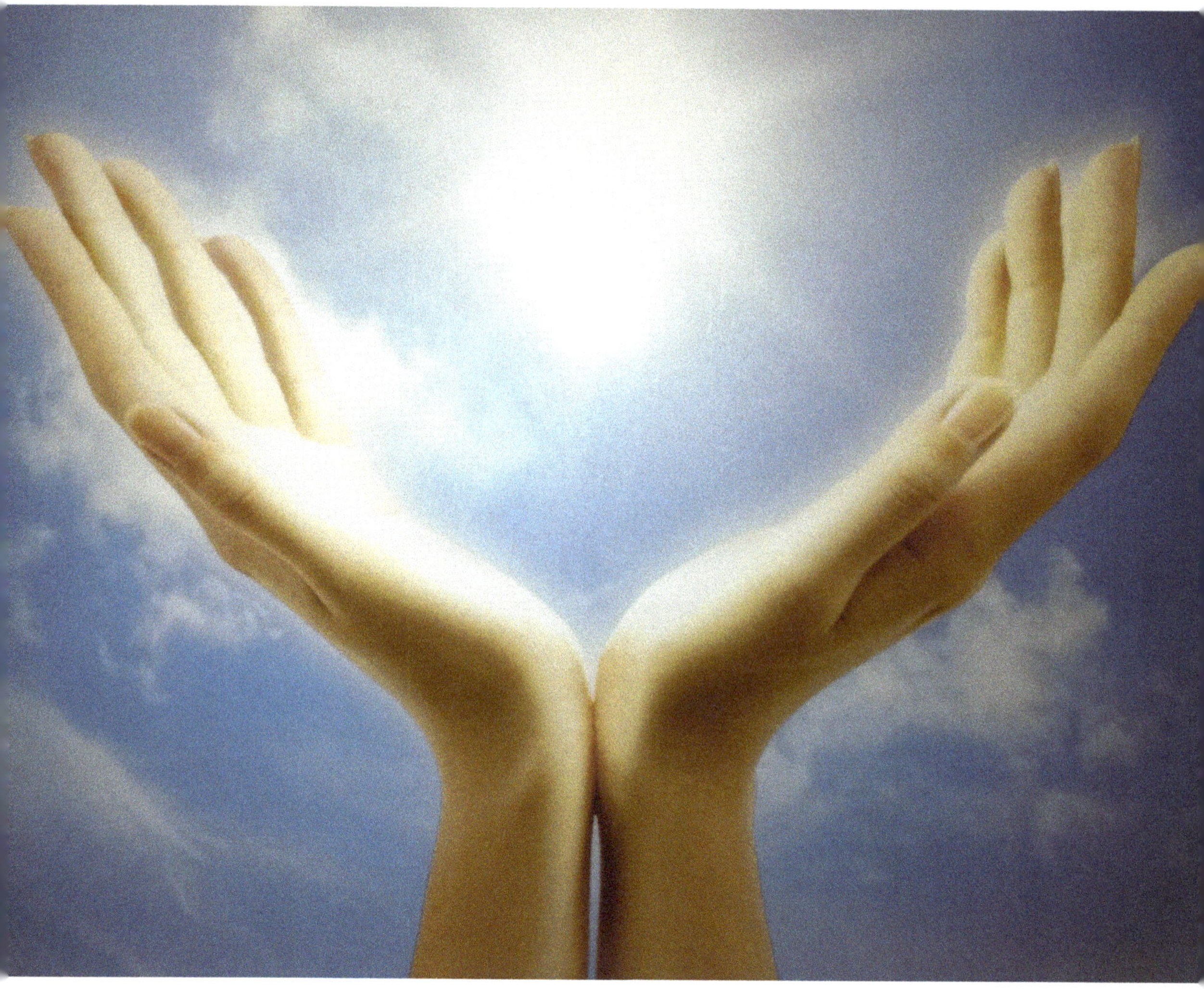

Stay Strong

When a family member or friend is sick, the first thing to do is to be as strong as you can for them. But by doing this, you need someone to be there for you because, talk about being physically and mentally drained; that can be an understatement. You can feel your own energy completely zapped right out of you, so you definitely need someone too. And try to get as much rest as you can, and meditate when you can. Also make sure you eat well. Try to eat a lot of healthy foods.

When you know that you've done the very best that you can for them, put it in God's hands because there are things that are beyond our control, and this is one of them. It's very hard to see a loved one very sick or dying, but by being there for them, that's all you can do. The rest is up to our creator, God. So turn it over to him.

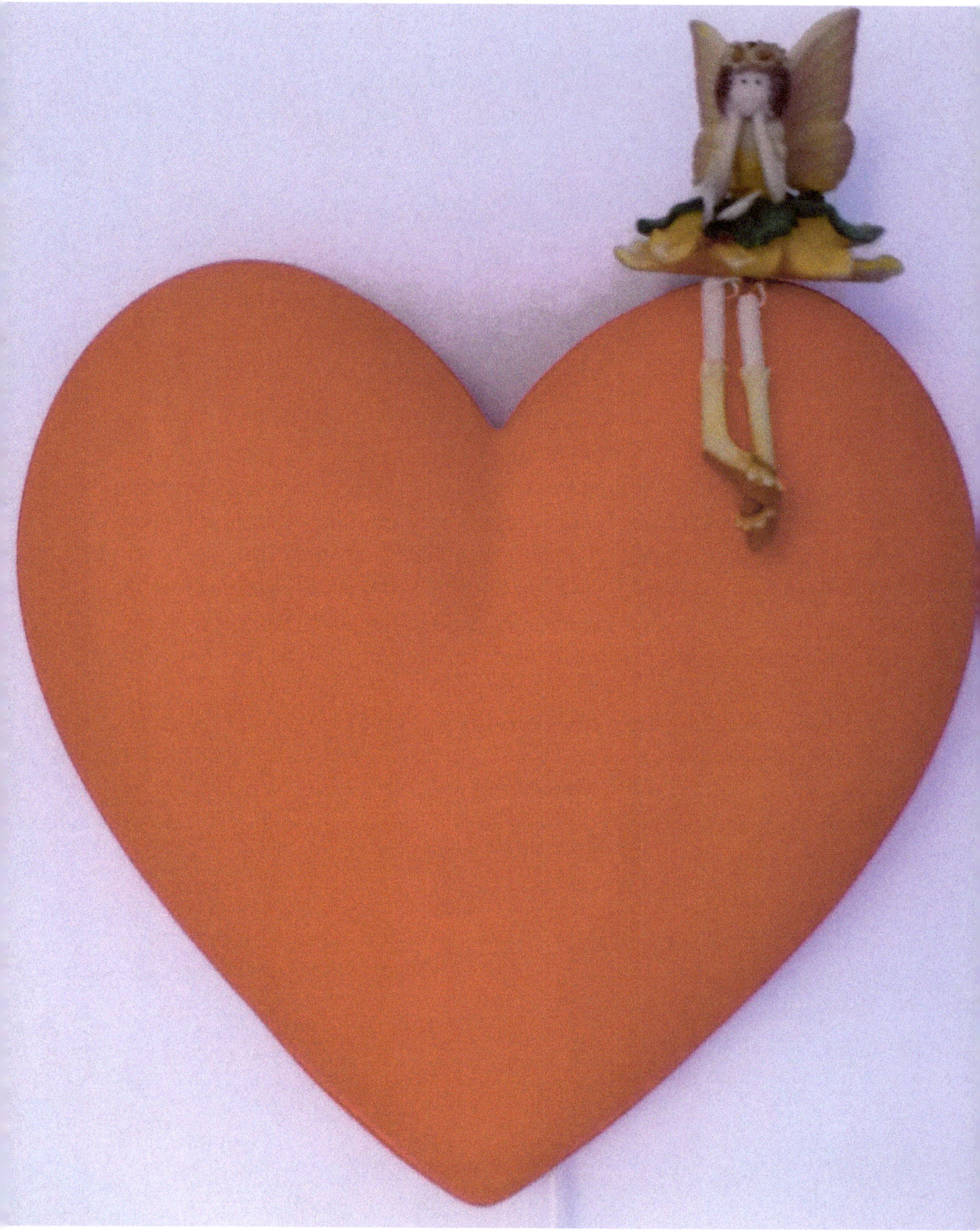

Love and Respect

Name a person in this world who does not want to be respected and loved. We all want people to be respectful, whether it's family, friends, or co-workers. Respect falls into all kinds of categories—respecting one's self, showing respect to others, and respecting other people's property. Let's not forget to respect Mother Nature. Sometimes, we really do take a lot of things for granted without even realizing that we are doing that. But we can only go on doing that up until a certain point, and then as they say, "something's got to give." That's when things start to happen, a chain of events that we will not be happy with.

So show some respect. Be respectful to yourself and to others. And yes, we all want to be loved. You would just be fooling yourself to say otherwise.

There are people who have all the money and fame, but are totally unhappy. They're doing drugs, drinking, and abusing themselves. Why? I bet they are looking for someone who will give them love and respect.

People get confused between love and sex. Sex is a moment; love is a lifetime. So share the love; show some respect. We all deserve it. Yes! Love is the answer.

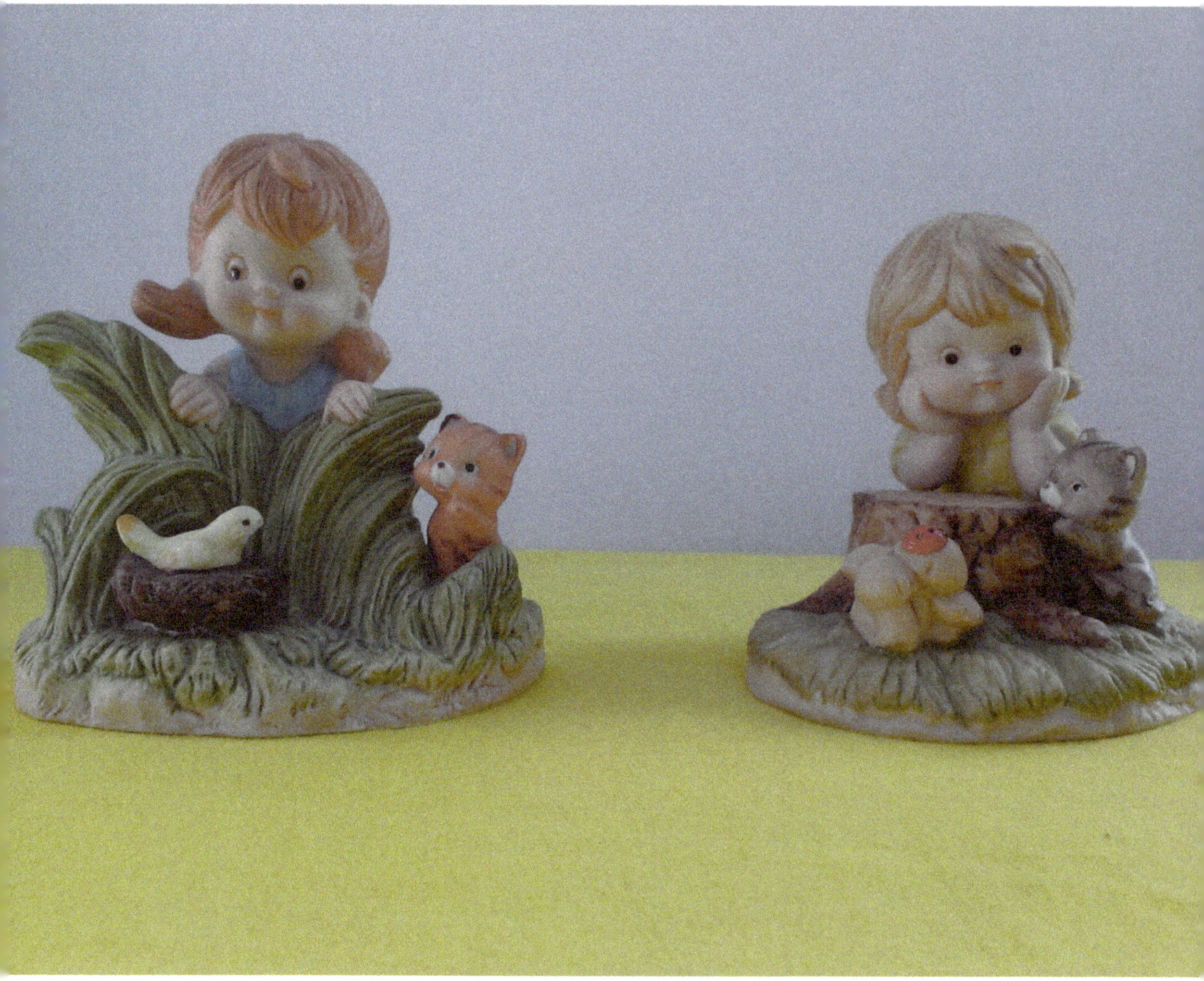

Focus on the Moment

Do you ever notice that when a special occasion comes up, we find ourselves worrying about all the details of the event—how it's going to be? is everything going to go all right that we sort of missed out on that day? Well, there a lot of us, who do this on a daily basis. For instance, we could be walking in the park, and instead of focusing on the beautiful scenery, we think about all the things we need to do when we get home. Or if we go on vacation, we might be thinking if everything back at the house is okay, if the dog is okay, or is this okay, is that okay. We have got to start training the brain to focus on the moment. It's like we are constantly multi-tasking our brain, and then we wonder why we get stressed and burnt out. Because for some of us, when we get the opportunity to relax and recharge, there goes the moment we start thinking about all the things we have to do. Let's not fall into that trap. So when the opportunity arises, when you feel the moment—absorb it. Like a sponge, soak it all in.

So focus on those great moments of life!

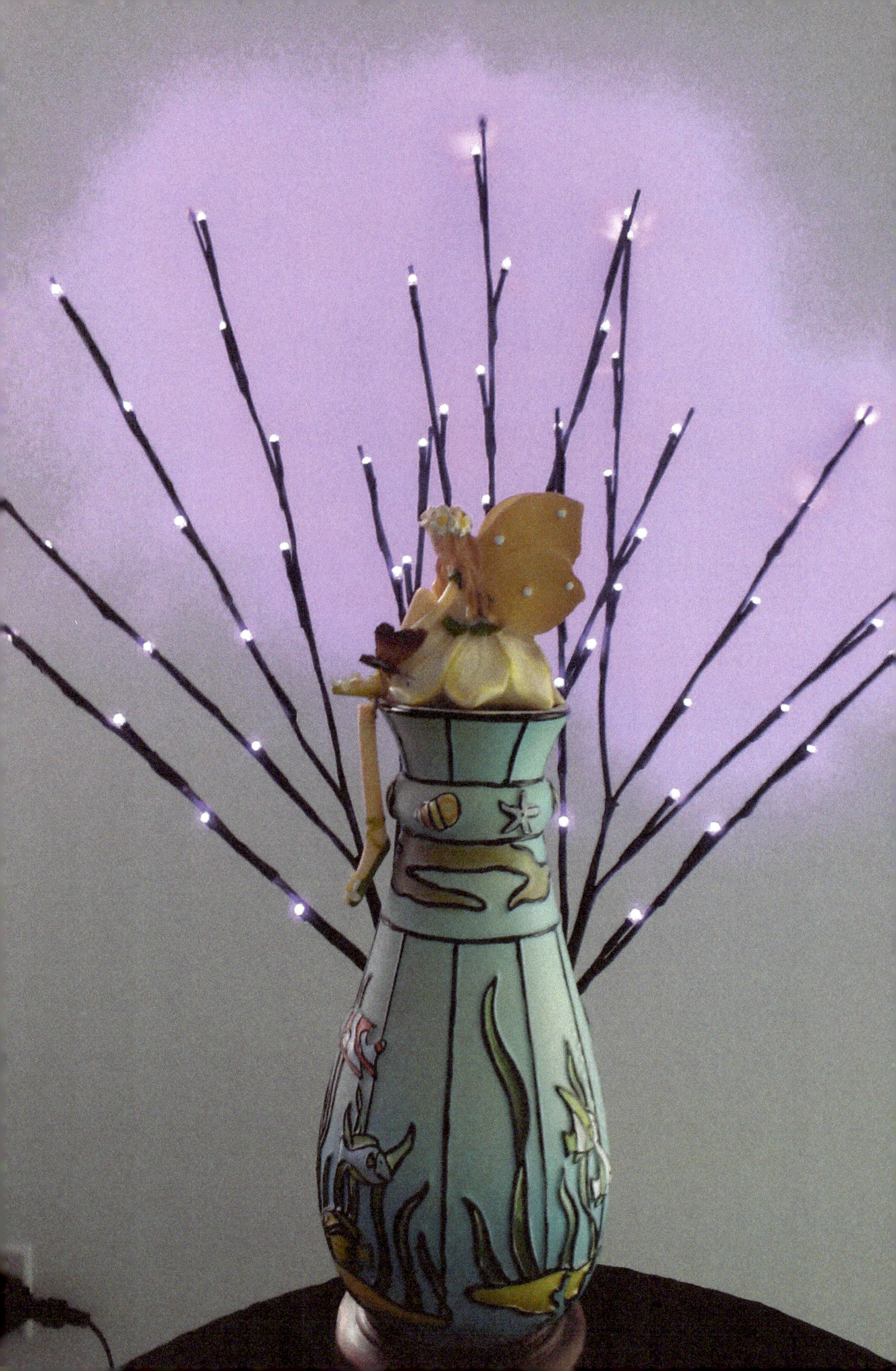

Genie Wish

If you had a genie and he granted you three wishes, what will they be? Think about that for a while. It is a really tricky question. Sometimes, the things we want or we think we want, once we get it, it's not what we thought it would be. You know that saying, "better be careful what you wish for."

Some people will say, "I wish to be happy." Okay, what is it that's going to make you happy? Is it more money, losing weight, own a home, or travel? By thinking about what our three wishes would be is answering the question to ourselves, "What is it that we really want or need, and what is truly going to make us happy?"

Sometimes, it's not knowing what we really want.

So I am giving you another assignment. What are the three wishes you will wish for?

And after you have your three wishes, work on making those wishes come true for yourself—one wish at a time.

>May all your wishes come true.
>Whether they're big or
>Whether they're small I
>Wish all the best for you.
>
>When we were kids, we wish
>When were adults, we do
>
>So do the things you
>Wish for, and may all
>Your wishes come true.

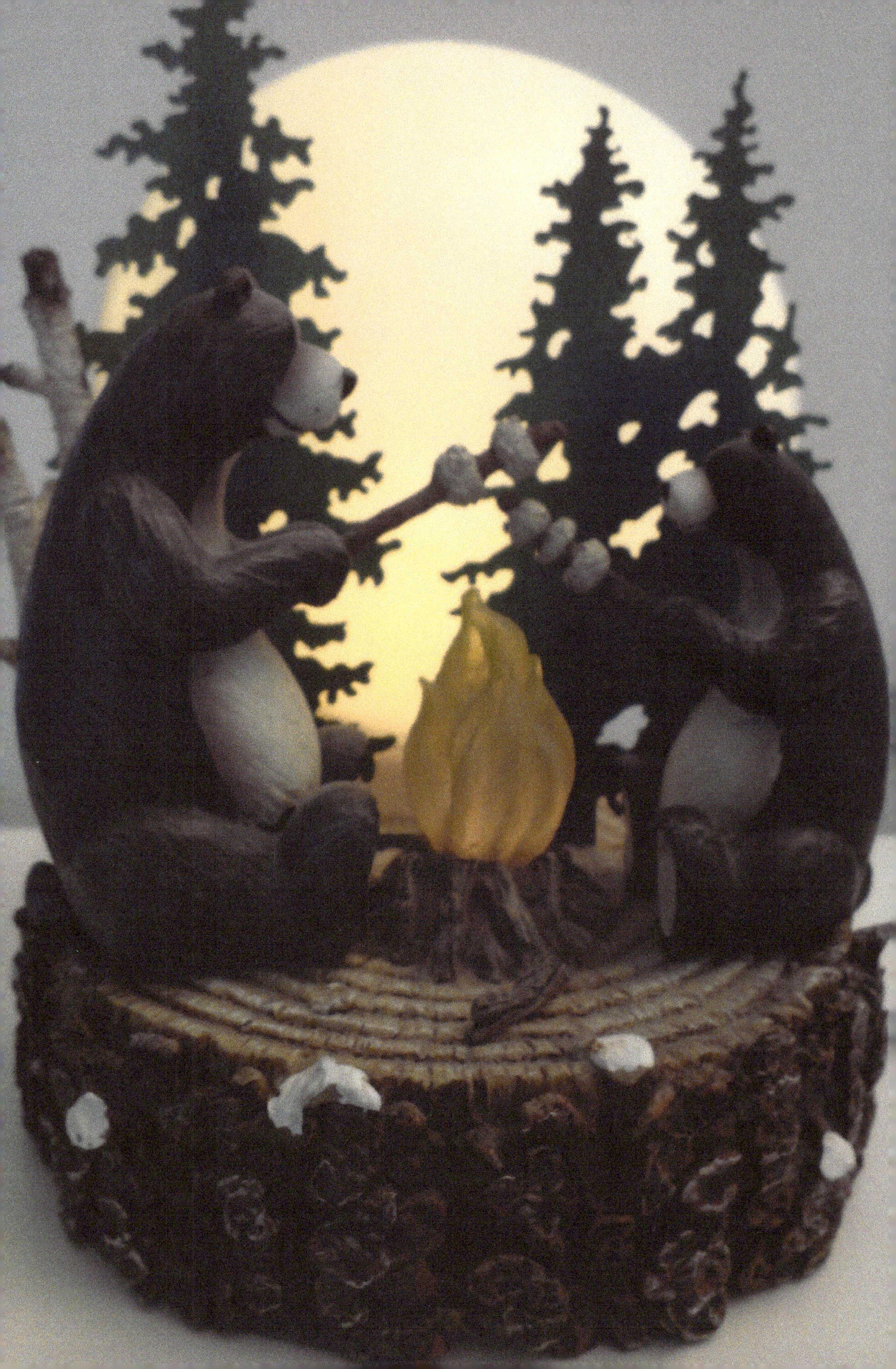

Trust

I think everyone can identify with this one. Sometimes, I actually feel like I am in a movie, where you ask, "Is he the good guy, or is he the bad guy?" Are you with me or are you against me?

Sometimes, when we got lied to so much, it's hard believing and trusting what other people have to say. They could be actually telling you the truth, but you don't believe them. It's like the story, "The Boy Who Cried Wolf." If you lie enough times, nobody is going to believe you. Their trust in you is gone, and that's something that's hard to get back.

Some people are very trusting, and when certain people find this out, unfortunately, some get taken advantage of.

Trust is something we have to earn.

Doctors and mechanics are high on the list. They need to earn your trust. Anyone who owns a car and had it repaired knows this. And if you don't trust your doctor, you could be in some big trouble.

Trust is very important.

We are living in the time, where trust has become a big issue. So sometimes, we have got to use our gut instincts.

And when we find people we can truly trust, it's like finding gold, but only better.

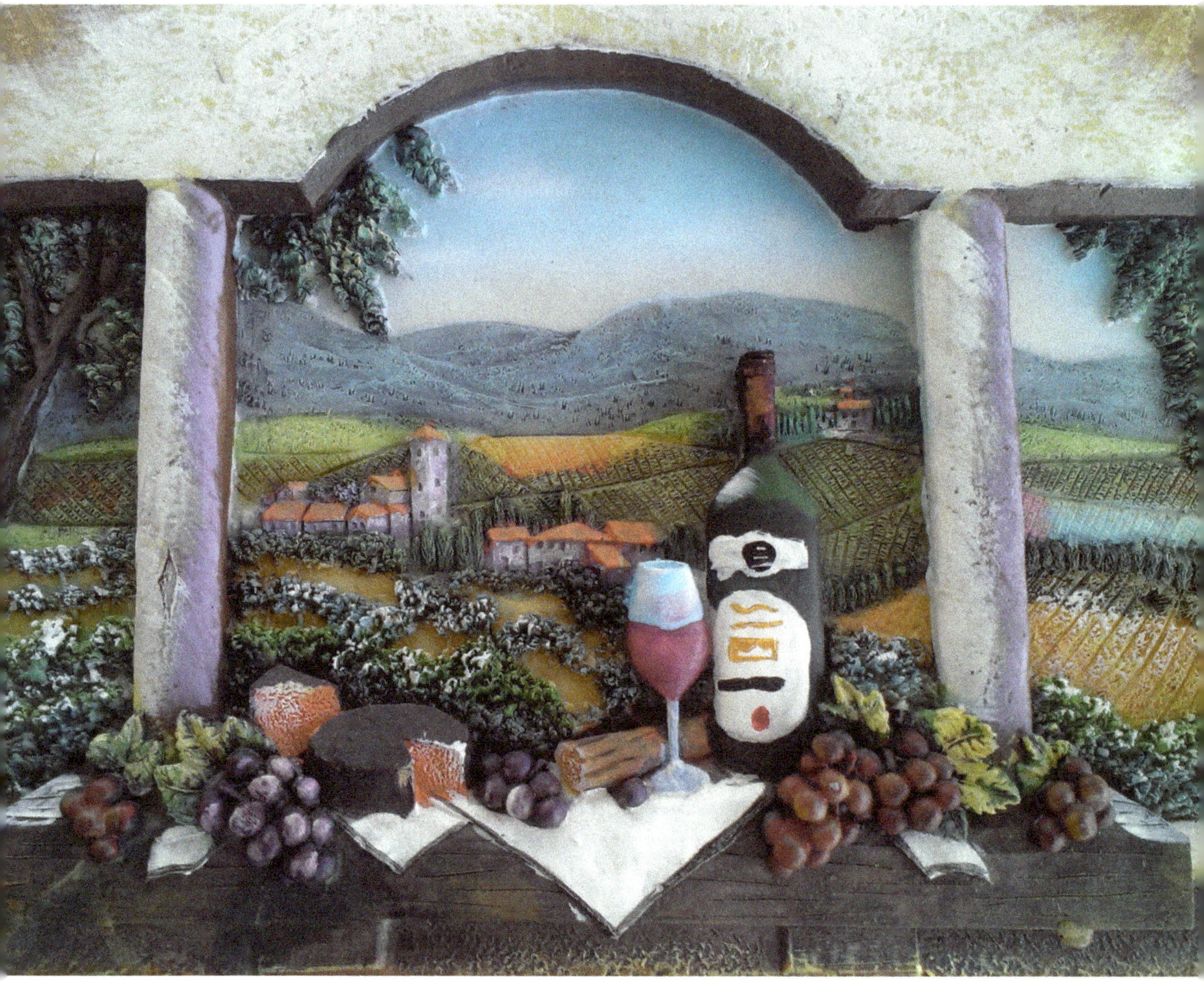

Enhance Your Life

Enhance your life by doing different things and going to different places. Make it a point to do five different things a year—things that you never tried, places you've never seen, or it could be eating different food.

Sometimes we fall into a pattern that we start getting used to doing—the same routine day after day, year after year.

We need to start changing it up a bit. Maybe there's a book that you never got a chance to read, or maybe you could try writing one. Learn a new dance; try yoga, tai chi, or meditation. Maybe learn a new language, or playing an instrument. Have you ever been on a cruise, seen the Grand Canyon, the Statue of Liberty. Maybe you have never been to Mackinaw Island, or went up into a light house, take a road trip across the United States and visit Graceland drive through the Smokey Mountains. The list goes on and on. You could have a lot of fun. Just try to figure out what your five amazing new things could be that you would like to achieve.

In our lives, it's very important to look forward to things. There are so many people who work so hard day in and day out. You have to take time to reward yourself for all the hard work that you do and for all the juggling to make everything work.

So even if it's on a smaller scale, try to find time to fit five fun, new, exciting, adventurous, and creative activities in your life. Be a child again. Put a sticker or star next to each one that you have accomplished.

So I think you know what I am going to ask of you. Yes, for you to start making your list right now. You will see that it will be a lot of fun for your family and friends

They will probably want to start making their own list too. It will be a lot of fun sharing ideas with one another.

Now there's your answer for reinventing yourself and enhancing your life—by keeping an open mind to things that might be foreign to us, and trying to live life to our fullest potential and challenging ourselves to things we might not be familiar with.

Change Your Mind Change Your Life

Someone once told me that the more you tell or ask somebody to do something, the more they're not going to do it. I find it sad to think that there would be people out there who would feel this way. Just imagine if we all did, would anything ever get done? Isn't that being a bit spiteful? Because maybe by them doing what you need them to do, it would make you happy. So is it because they don't want to see you happy and grateful for their help? If the shoe is on the other foot, wouldn't it make them happy when people do what they need them to do?

Then you got the same person saying you should have told me I would have fixed that.

The point is, if I don't ask you, you will say, "Why didn't you ask me? I would have done it," and if you do ask them, they'll say, "I don't want to do it."

It's interesting how some people look at situations and life differently. They have a different mindset. I think the only way people with this mindset will change, is when it starts happening to them. And maybe it will start to dawn on them, this is not a great way to go through life, talk about mind games and complicating your life.

Some of us really do make life a lot more stressful. With this way of thinking, it's a damn if you do and damn if you don't. There is no winning with them, and there's no talking to them either. They're right and you're wrong. If all of this sounds familiar to you, you need to back off or you'll find yourself getting very hurt and frustrated if you don't.

Now, on the other hand, if you feel that you act in this manner; it's a wake-up call to you. I don't think you want to be that kind of person.

So if we all would start changing, our thinking, and be aware of this in other people and ourselves, we could change our lives as well as everyone around us. Be the person whom people would want to hang around with and who enjoys your company.

So start changing your mind on some of these issues because I know it will change your life!

Looking Good!   How Wonderful!

You Are Beautiful!

Thank You!   Great Job!   I'm impressed

I could not have done it without you

Wow, you're amazing!

Compliments and Gratefulness Go a Long Way

A very important gesture in life is giving compliments. I think a lot of people tend to overlook this. People can be really quick to tell you that you didn't do a good job or they don't like how you did it. But when you do a great job and it turns out perfect, people have a tendency to overlook that, why is that?

I had called up the village by my house and told them the tree cutting team did a great job. She actually said, I don't know how to respond and then she said thank you. She said that I was the first person to ever call like that. She said the only calls they ever get are people complaining.

Case in point, when people do good deeds or a job well done let them know, that would really mean a lot to them.

Show that you are appreciative of their services. What a fantastic feeling they would get from people who do.

And who doesn't want to hear a compliment? If a person gets their hair done or they're wearing a nice outfit, tell them you like it. Be generous with giving compliments. I don't think there's a person on the planet that would not appreciate someone telling them how great they look or what a great job they have done.

Let's also not forget to stop taking people for granted. Because when you do, the hurt starts to develop and then the other person, soon becomes not so eager to want to help you. There might come a time when you desperately might need their help.

So let people know how important they are and don't just assume they know you are happy with their work.

Tell them. They would really love to hear it from you.

So everyday find things to compliment people on.

And start appreciating the things that people do for you and let's not take people for granted. Because if you do, one day they just might not be there for you.

So brighten up someone's day just by saying:

"Wow! What a great job and you are amazing."

People will love you for that.

Spread the love.

And Now What

I want you to visualize yourself having everything you could possible want, go ahead and really put it all out there. An unbelievable home, incredible cars, travel all over the world have lots of money, whatever you could imagine becomes your reality, now what are you thinking?

I will tell you what I am thinking; three words show up vividly in my mind. And now, what.

Some people, when they have everything, start saying: seen it, been there, done that. Some have a tendency to become a little bored with life.

So it got me to thinking, if someone hands you over everything you could possible want, you would be truly missing out.

It would be one of the biggest injustices of life. To not have had the feeling of accomplishment, the journey, the struggles, the achievement, meeting some incredible people along the way.

All of these build character. Make us more understanding of others and for the jobs they do. We must realize, we are all important.

Here's another scenario. Some people say I'm going to sell everything and move to an island. I'm going to sit on the balcony every day and look out at the ocean. I think that's absolutely wonderful for a while, and then my three words ring out like a bell.

And Now What.

We all know how sitting too long is not a healthy idea, and how important it is to stay busy. What gets some of us in trouble is, we stop growing and start making excuses.

So even if it's small goals, little tasks, little achievements. Don't ever stop growing, learning, and staying busy.

I have a saying that I say after I had a very busy day, and I got a lot of work accomplished; I say, "I deserve the couch." I actually feel a bit guilty if I didn't do all the things I would have liked to have gotten done for the day. And then I say, "I don't deserve the couch."

This is the long and the short of it.

It's great to have, but it's even greater to achieve not get things handed over to us. And that we live a meaningful and purposeful life that we take the journey, getting through the struggles, and going down the path where you read the sign that says: and now what.

And you will know that you deserve to be there because you've earned it.

But the special meaning to all of this is, be ready for the what comes after, don't ever stop finding things to do, just don't overdo it. Balance your day.

Don't ever look at it as finished, but a beginning to a new adventure.

So before you get to that point in your life, where you say: and now what. You better start making out your list today. So you can be prepared for the next incredible stage of your life, you have the wisdom, the power, the control. You are now in the driver's seat, fasten your seatbelt and away we go.

So what are you passionate about? What are your hobbies? Don't forget to put volunteer on the list.

This will be the list that you could fulfill when you get to that question.

And now what, what should I do. You will have your answer. But you will know its all up to you!

And now that you're all done reading. Go ahead and pass it on. Be a leader and not a follower. Lead the way to freedom. To free yourself from all the things that have been keeping you down.

Because now, you know you have the power and control, but remember to use self-control. And you hold the key to making things happen.

So unlock the door and open it up. It's amazing what you might find there. But just remember: <u>No one else can do it for you</u>. It's your journey, it's your life. So love your life, it is a gift from God.

You can lead a horse to water, but you can't make him drink it. Go ahead drink the water God would want you to, and turn off the TV and while you're at it, shut the computer down, turn your cell phone off, and go outside take a walk, listen to the birds.

Go to the park, sit by a river, lake, or a pond. Get in touch with Mother Nature. What a beautiful site.

There's something to be said with living simple and less is more. We surround ourselves with a lot of stuff and some of us way too much stuff. But what does it all really mean? So much of that stuff we never use, and that can start weighing us down.

So let's start traveling a little lighter. Less to take care of and more time to enjoy life.

Life, Love, and You
It's a Beautiful Thing!

God bless you
and God truly does love each and every one of us.

Thank You

I don't know who you are, but now you know me. I just want to say thank you with love to you from me. The answers can be found; they are hidden in our hearts.

It's truly up to us to work our problems out. Yes, it's a puzzle. It's the game of life. But we all have the choice to choose, to do what we know is right. So send love throughout the universe and, yes, it will come back, providing that you go down the love and caring path.

So thank you for reading my book. It's written simply but it's true from a simple girl.

With love from me to you.

Love,
Louise

Special Thanks

I want to give a
A special thanks to
My incredible husband,
Charlie, on being here
With me through this
Amazing journey of life

To my caring and loving
Children, Lisa and Paul
And to their spouses.
My son-in-law, Jeremy, and
My daughter-in-law, Renee

To my grandson, Benjamin
Who's my big sports star
Whether it's golf, baseball
Or floor hockey, Great Job Ben.
To my new beautiful
Baby granddaughter, Micky
Welcome to the world

To my Mother, Mary Lou,
Who I learned a lot from
Life is a learning experience

My sister, Linda, for working
With me through the challenges
That life throws at us

To the rest of my family
And my husband's family
Friends and neighbors
We really do learn a lot
From each other and
Just knowing that your
There for us is
absolutely wonderful.

Thank you.

The following are songs that I wrote from the past.

I lose control whenever you're near me
So much passion I feel for you
I just can't hide the way that I feel
Something happens when I get next to you

Hold me tight
All through the night
Squeeze me, please me
But just don't tease me

Hold me tight
It feels so right
When you hold me tight

Repeat First Verse

Repeat Chorus

Written by Louise Howe
1990

Don't Play with My Heart

You got me so confused
I just don't know what to do
You better stop playing around
You know you're bringing me down
It's time to get serious
Tell me what you wanna do
So don't change the subject
Hey, I'm talkin' to you

Don't play with my heart
Finish what you started
Don't say I love you
Then tell me that we are through
You got to make-up your mind
You're running out of time
Don't play with my heart
You got to finish what you started

You better stop playing games
Stop wastin' my time
Honey just be straight with me
Are you just lookin' for a good time?
I always thought that you care for
Well I guess I was wrong
I can't stand to be hurt no more
So baby, so long

Repeat Chorus

I'm gonna take some action
I'll I get some satisfaction
Is it love your looking for?
Or are you after something more?
I just don't understand it
Why you treat me so cruel?
There's one more thing I got to say
I still think I love you

Repeat chorus

Don't play with my heart
You've got to finish what you started
Don't play with my heart
You've got to finish what you started

Written by Louis Howe
1990

Lonely is the Night

Louise Howe

Lonely is the night without you
Feeling like a fool waiting for you
Feelin' the way I do
I will always love—you

My nights they seem so long
Whenever you are, gone
Tell me it's not true
I heard you found somebody new
Tell me it's not true
I can't get over losing you
And like a fool I'm waiting for you

Lonely is the night without you—
Feeling like a fool waiting for you
Feelin' the way I do
I will always want—you

I can't get over you
No matter what I do think
About you day and night
My love for you it feels so right
Think about you day and night
So come on back and love me tonight
So come on back and love me tonight

How lonely it can be
When you're not here with me
My nights they've been so blue
I'm lonely without you

Feeling the way I do
I will always love—you

All I do is think about you
I don't want to ever lose you
You mean so much to me
Bring your love back here to me
You mean so much to me
So bring love back here to me
So bring your love
So bring your love
Back here to me

Lonely is the night without you
Feeling like a fool wanting for you
Feelin' the way I do
I will always want—you

Lonely is the night without you
Feelin' like a fool waiting for you
Lonely is the night without you
I don't want to ever love you

Repeat Out

© 1987

I am very happy to have finally written my book. It was one of my "genie wishes" and Page Publishing made it come true.

Thank you, Page Publishing.

Special thanks to:
Richard Roma
Nichole Hoffman

Dreams really can come true!

About the Author

I was born and raised in Chicago. I have two sisters, Linda and Theresa, and a half-brother by the name of Jimmy. Life was definitely not easy growing up. It had its challenges. Somehow it's amazing how we can overcome things. You have to learn to be creative. We grew up pretty fast back in the day. We did a lot of walking and taking the bus. We didn't have very much so what we got we took care of and appreciated everything we would get.

I can remember taking the 26th street bus to downtown State Street to go shopping by myself with the money I made from babysitting and cleaning the neighbor's house. I was only ten years old at that time. Nobody knew that's what I did, because of course they would not have let me go. But it was a great adventure.

I was pretty mature for my age. I got married at the age of 19 to an incredible guy by the name of Charlie. Two years later I had my first child, Lisa, and two weeks after that we opened up a small business. It was a shoe store. Four and a half years later I had my son Paul. We had the shoe store for ten years.

I started selling Avon products for a while and then started singing and writing songs. I went on to sing in clubs, car shows, and different events. I met some amazing people. I got to see both sides of the coin. What I mean by that is, the people at home with the family thinking they're missing out on the nightlife and some people at the clubs wishing they were married and had a family. I was a mother and housewife during the week and a singer on the weekends. Life really is a balancing act. We try to do the best we can with what we are given.

I have a grandson by the name of Benjamin and he is twelve years old. He is growing up to be a fantastic young man. My daughter Lisa, and her husband, Jeremy, can be very proud of him. My son, Paul, and his wife Renee just had a beautiful baby girl by the name of Micky. I am sure they are going to be great parents. What a great addition she will be to the family.

Now, for me in my life, deep down inside I always wanted to write a book about life. We go to school to learn math, science, etc., but what about life? It's great to be book-smart but with that, you better have some common sense to go along with it. I think children at an early age need to know they have the control but to use it wisely, because the decisions they make can and will affect them the rest of their lives. Not to mention it can have devastating effects on the rest of the family if they choose to make bad choices.

CPSIA information can be obtained
at www.ICGtesting.com
Printed in the USA
LVHW02s1020151217
559658LV00008B/14/P